Phil Collins

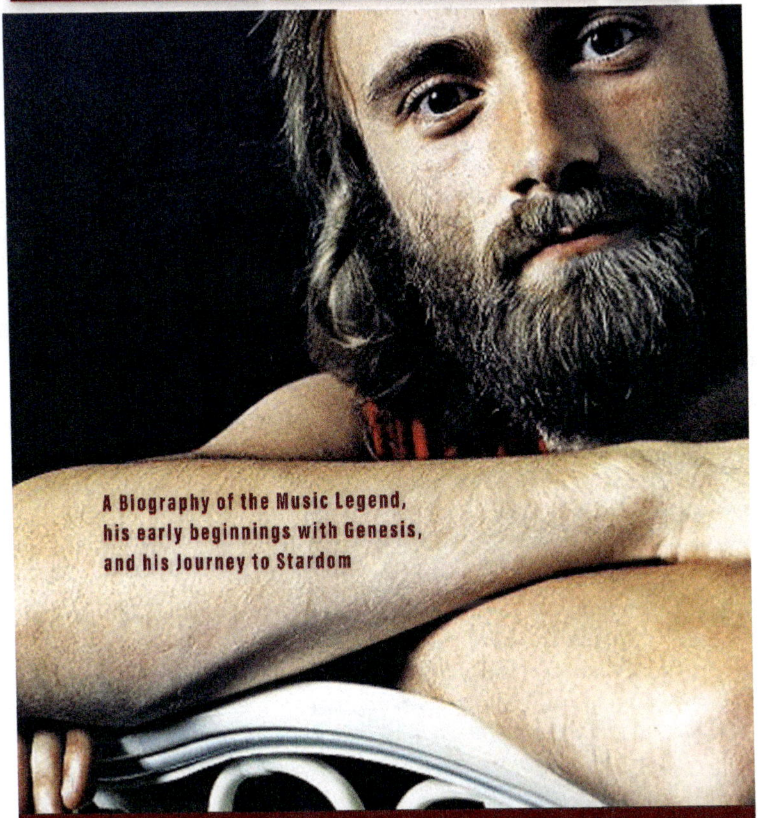

A Biography of the Music Legend,
his early beginnings with Genesis,
and his Journey to Stardom

David V. Legend

Acknowledgments

Writing a biography of someone as iconic as Phil Collins is both a privilege and a responsibility, and I am deeply grateful to those who have supported and guided me throughout this journey.

First and foremost, my heartfelt thanks go to Phil Collins himself. His music has been a constant source of inspiration, and the opportunity to delve into his incredible journey from Genesis to global stardom has been a rewarding and humbling experience. I am in awe of his artistry, his impact on music, and the legacy he has created, which continues to resonate with generations of fans.

To the band Genesis, whose groundbreaking work laid the foundation for Phil Collins' musical career, your innovation and creativity have changed the course of rock and pop history forever. Thank you for your music, which is the heart of this story.

I must extend my gratitude to the many biographers, journalists, and music historians whose previous work provided invaluable insight into Phil Collins' life and career. Your research and dedication to preserving the history of music are deeply appreciated.

A special thank you to the fans of both Phil Collins and Genesis. Your passion, loyalty, and unwavering support are what have kept the music alive, inspiring me every day as I wrote this book.

To my editor, whose sharp eye and keen insight shaped this manuscript into its final form, thank you for your invaluable contributions. You have my deepest appreciation for your tireless effort in making this book the best it could be. To my friends and family, thank you for your patience and encouragement throughout the writing process. Your belief in me kept me going even on the toughest days.

Finally, to anyone who reads this book: Thank you for sharing in the celebration of Phil Collins' remarkable life and musical journey. I hope that this biography will not only honor his legacy but also introduce new generations of fans to the music that has shaped so many lives.

David V. Legend

Table of contents

Introduction
SETTING THE STAGE FOR A LEGEND

In the world of music, there are few names as synonymous with the sound and spirit of an era as Phil Collins. Whether you first encountered his voice through the ethereal, haunting tones of "In the Air Tonight" or saw him drumming with an intensity that was as much about passion as technique in the iconic group Genesis, there's no denying the mark he has left on both pop and rock music. Over the decades, Phil Collins has not only shaped the sound of two generations, but his music has touched listeners across the globe, transcending borders, genres, and time.

Phil Collins' journey, both as a member of Genesis and as a solo artist, has been nothing short of extraordinary. Born into the sprawling cultural revolution of the 1960s, he emerged in the 1970s as a young, eager musician, and by the 1980s, he was at the helm of an international phenomenon, effortlessly moving between the hard-edged sounds of rock and the smooth, commercial territory of pop. His unique ability to blend both styles made him a true bridge between two musical worlds, but it was his unmistakable voice and drumming style that solidified his position as a towering figure in popular music history.

This biography of Phil Collins aims to trace the evolution of this musical icon. It will follow him through the early, formative years with Genesis, chart his rise to superstardom, and then explore the highs and lows of his solo career. The aim is to capture not only the man but the music, exploring the pivotal moments in his life that defined both his career and the cultural shifts that followed in his wake. From his first steps into the world of music to his enduring legacy today, we will delve into the intricate layers of Collins' life, career, and the unforgettable soundtracks he created.

The Early Days: A Musical Beginning in the Cultural Revolution

To truly understand Phil Collins' impact on the world of music, one must first consider the time and place in which he was born. Collins grew up in a post-war London, a city in the throes of profound cultural and musical change. The 1960s had already set the stage for a revolution, both in terms of technology and artistic freedom. In a world where the Beatles, the Rolling Stones, and later, Pink Floyd, were shaping the landscape of music, London was a mecca for young artists eager to make their mark.

However, the musical revolution was not one of overnight success. It was built on decades of innovation, experimentation, and, often, struggle. The 1970s were an interesting time for the British music scene. While mainstream pop music became more polished and commercial, a counterculture of musicians sought to break free from convention, searching for new sounds, new forms of expression. It was in this environment that Collins found his calling. At a young age, he was drawn to music, particularly the drums, and his interest in rhythm, sound, and performance grew with each passing year. From the very beginning, Collins was part of a generation that sought to break away from the formulaic, to carve out a new space for raw emotion and innovative sound.

As a teenager, Collins immersed himself in the music of the day, but his roots were firmly planted in rock and progressive rock, genres that demanded not just technical skill but also artistic expression. Collins was drawn to the ambitious musicality of bands like King Crimson and Yes, and it wasn't long before he started honing his skills in the local music scene, dreaming of being part of something larger.

In 1970, after some initial stints with bands in the British underground scene, Collins' path took a crucial turn. He auditioned for Genesis, a band on the rise but still struggling to find its identity. The group, formed in the late 1960s by keyboardist Tony Banks, guitarist Mike Rutherford, and vocalist Peter Gabriel, had yet to achieve mainstream success. The addition of Collins, who became their drummer, was a transformative one. While his technical ability on the drums was undeniable, it was his emotional depth and energy that became a defining feature of Genesis' sound.

The Rise of Genesis: A Band Transformed

The first years with Genesis were a study in growth and evolution. Genesis, initially known for its complex, layered, and often fantastical music, was beginning to find its footing. Collins's ability to adapt to the band's sound, while simultaneously influencing its direction, became integral to their development. Collins wasn't just a drummer; he was a storyteller, and his musical narrative added a crucial dimension to the band's evolving compositions.

Genesis was never a band to shy away from experimentation, and by the time Collins had fully cemented his role in the group, they were blending rock, jazz, and classical elements into something that felt completely new. Genesis's sound during this period—characterized by intricate melodies, sophisticated structures, and poetic lyrics—was immediately distinctive. They became pioneers of progressive rock, an evolving genre that sought to push boundaries and defy expectations.

But it was not just the music of Genesis that gained attention in the early 1970s. Collins' theatrical presence, his charisma behind the drums, and his growing role as a vocalist helped to set the band apart. While Peter Gabriel's mystical performances were undoubtedly part of the band's appeal, it was Collins' unique ability to create tension and release in the music that made Genesis feel alive.

Genesis would experience several evolutions during Collins' tenure, moving from progressive rock to a more commercial pop-rock sound. This shift was not just a reflection of the band's musical development; it mirrored a broader transformation in the musical landscape. The 1980s, in particular, would become a time of immense personal and professional growth for Collins, as he would find himself at the crossroads of his band's success and his solo ambitions.

The Solo Years: Breaking Out Into a Solo Career

Phil Collins had always been the heart of Genesis, but as the band began to gain more commercial success, it became clear that he had much more to offer beyond his role as the band's drummer and occasional vocalist. In 1981, he released *Face Value*, his first solo album, which would go on to become a massive success. The album was a departure from his work with Genesis, marked by more personal, introspective songs and the unforgettable hit "In the Air Tonight."

The song itself became a cultural touchstone, with its haunting beats and emotionally charged lyrics captivating listeners worldwide. Collins could blend raw emotion with a meticulous musical sensibility that made him stand out as an artist in his own right. And while Genesis was continuing to evolve, Collins was beginning to forge his path as a solo artist, creating music that was accessible yet deeply personal.

The success of *Face Value* opened the door for more solo work, and Collins quickly became a global music sensation.

Albums like *No Jacket Required* and *...But Seriously* solidified his place as one of the leading figures of the 1980s and 1990s music scene. Collins had become more than just the drummer of Genesis; he had become a cultural icon, one whose songs were played on radios and in living rooms around the world.

As his solo career flourished, Collins faced the challenge of maintaining his position in Genesis, navigating the delicate balance between being part of a band that had given him so much and pursuing his artistic vision. Despite this, he managed to straddle both worlds, bringing his energy and passion to both his solo work and the collaborative efforts of Genesis.

Purpose of the Biography

This biography is an exploration of Phil Collins, a man whose life is inextricably linked to the music of his time. His journey from humble beginnings to global superstardom is not just a tale of fame and success; it is a testament to the enduring power of music to connect people, to speak to their hearts, and to define eras.

Through this book, we will trace Collins' roots in Genesis, explore his rise to prominence, and examine his profound influence on popular culture. We will reflect on the struggles, the triumphs, and the personal stories that have shaped the man behind the music. His career has spanned decades and has weathered the winds of change, yet his voice—whether through his drum kit, his songwriting, or his powerful vocals—remains a constant in the musical world.

This biography is not only a journey through the highs and lows of an artist's life, but also a deeper exploration of the cultural movements that influenced his music and, in turn, how his music has influenced the world around him. Phil Collins' impact on the music industry and fans worldwide is undeniable. His songs have become the soundtrack to countless lives, capturing the emotions of a generation.

In the chapters that follow, we will explore the life of Phil Collins, beginning with his early days in Genesis, tracing his rise to stardom, and reflecting on the profound legacy he has created in the world of music. This is the story of a man who didn't just make music—he made history.

Chapter 1
THE GENESIS OF A LEGEND
1.1 Early Life and Musical Beginnings

Phil Collins was born on January 30, 1951, in the bustling metropolis of London, a city whose streets were alive with the echoes of change. As the world emerged from the shadow of World War II, the cultural landscape was rapidly shifting, with music playing a pivotal role in reshaping society. The 1960s and 1970s were particularly formative years for those like Collins, who were coming of age amid the cultural revolution that would come to define their generation.

For Collins, the seed of his musical journey was planted early. His parents, Winifred and Greville Collins, were both middle-class and non-musical, but they recognized early on that their son had an extraordinary passion for music. Growing up in Chiswick, West London, Phil found solace in the art of rhythm and melody. His interest in music began, as it often does for many young people, with an infectious enthusiasm for popular sounds. The British invasion had brought acts like The Beatles, The Rolling Stones, and The Kinks to the forefront, and it was these artists who shaped the cultural DNA of his youth.

As a child, Collins was drawn to his family's record collection, mesmerized by the sounds of Elvis Presley, The Beatles, and Motown. His fascination with rhythm began with the simplest of instruments—his hands. He was frequently found tapping on whatever surface he could find—tables, chairs, even the backs of cars—practicing rudimentary drumming patterns. His obsession with rhythm soon found an outlet when he was given his first drum kit at the age of 14. It was a modest set, yet for Collins, it was a treasure trove, opening up a new world of creative possibilities.

Before long, Phil had immersed himself in drumming, refining his technique and discovering the drummers who would inspire his style. Charlie Watts of The Rolling Stones and Ringo Starr of The Beatles were the early idols who shaped his musical taste. But it was the unique drumming style of jazz legend Buddy Rich that would leave a lasting impact. Collins studied Rich's precision and speed with an almost academic reverence, and it wasn't long before he began to form his own ideas about what a drummer could achieve within a band. He recognized the power of percussion as not just a rhythmic support but as a central force in driving the emotional intensity of a song.

Phil's path, however, was not an easy one. The Collins family did not have the means to support his burgeoning musical career, and Phil knew that his dreams could only be realized through grit, perseverance, and a touch of good fortune. At age 14, he auditioned for the famous stage musical *Oliver!*, and against the odds, he won the role of the Artful Dodger. It was his first taste of professional performance, and it cemented his desire to pursue music as a career.

But despite his growing passion for drumming, Collins faced the uncertainty that many aspiring musicians experience: the world of professional music was a cutthroat, competitive place, and there were no guarantees. He honed his craft by joining various local bands, each one contributing to his growth. But it was not until a serendipitous moment in 1970 that his life would change forever.

1.2 Joining Genesis: The Start of an Era
In 1970, Genesis was still a relatively unknown band, struggling to find their identity within the highly competitive London music scene. Founded by keyboardist Tony Banks, guitarist Mike Rutherford, and lead singer Peter Gabriel, Genesis had spent several years working on their sound but

had yet to achieve mainstream recognition. They were a progressive rock band with lofty ambitions—blending elements of classical music, folk, and rock in complex, intricate compositions.

The band was in need of a new drummer after their previous drummer, John Mayhew, left due to creative differences. Collins, whose style had matured over the years, was not a typical choice for a progressive rock band. He was young, energetic, and lacked a lengthy pedigree. However, after auditioning for Genesis, Collins quickly impressed the band members with his precision, musicality, and passion. He became the group's new drummer, joining Genesis just as they were on the cusp of an evolution that would change the course of their career.

In the early days, Collins wasn't just a drummer—he was a vital part of the band's core, contributing to the intricate musical landscapes they created. The complexity of Genesis' music demanded not just a technically skilled drummer but someone who could think beyond mere percussion, crafting patterns that would complement the band's wide-ranging sound. Collins' technical prowess allowed him to lock in with the band's intricate rhythms while also adding his own distinctive voice to the band's sound.

The first album he contributed to with Genesis was *Nursery Cryme* (1971), a bold, sprawling work that highlighted the band's unique approach to progressive rock. The album's standout tracks—such as "The Musical Box" and "The Return of the Giant Hogweed"—showcased Collins' ability to play in complex time signatures while maintaining the fluidity and emotion that Genesis' music demanded.

However, despite their talent and musical innovation, Genesis was still not an instant success. The band struggled with securing mainstream recognition, and their music was too experimental for the tastes of many casual listeners. The concept albums, intricate lyrics, and long instrumental passages were the stuff of cult followings, not radio hits. Genesis spent several years navigating the uncertainty of the music industry, working tirelessly to perfect their sound and garner attention from major record labels.

As a band, Genesis went through several changes in lineup and sound during the early years, but it was their live performances that truly captured the attention of fans.

Collins' drumming was hypnotic, an unstoppable force that matched the band's ambitious compositions. He added an emotional weight to the music that resonated with fans in a way that few drummers could. In addition to his drumming, Collins began to take on more vocal duties in the band, which ultimately marked the beginning of his evolution as a frontman.

The turning point for Genesis came in 1974 with the release of *The Lamb Lies Down on Broadway*, a double concept album that is now considered one of the band's masterpieces. This album, a sprawling narrative about a young Puerto Rican named Rael, marked a significant moment in Genesis' history. It solidified the band as one of the leading figures of the progressive rock movement. While Peter Gabriel was still the band's charismatic frontman, Collins' drumming was now a key component of the band's sound.

However, despite the success of *The Lamb Lies Down on Broadway*, the internal dynamics of the band began to shift. Gabriel, the band's theatrical and enigmatic frontman, was growing increasingly disillusioned with the pressures of being in Genesis. The band's elaborate stage shows and intense creative demands were beginning to wear on him. In 1975, Gabriel left the band, leaving the future of Genesis uncertain.

It was then that Collins, who had gradually emerged as the band's second vocalist, stepped into the spotlight. With Gabriel's departure, Collins became the lead singer of Genesis, effectively assuming the role of both drummer and frontman. His transition from a supporting member to the band's primary vocalist was not without its challenges, but it marked the beginning of a new era for Genesis.

1.3 The Struggles Before Stardom

Despite Collins stepping up as the new lead vocalist, Genesis faced significant struggles in the years following Gabriel's departure. The band was still wrestling with their identity, trying to maintain the complexity and grandeur of their earlier sound while adapting to a more radio-friendly format. The challenge was even more pronounced given that they were now without Gabriel's theatrical presence, which had been a crucial part of their appeal.

The 1976 album *A Trick of the Tail* marked Genesis's first release without Gabriel, and it was a critical and commercial success. The album showcased the band's ability to innovate and evolve, with tracks like "Dance on a Volcano" and "Los Endos" reflecting a mix of complex compositions and accessibility. Collins proved that he could carry the band both as a drummer and a vocalist, and the album was well-received by critics and fans alike.

Despite this success, the band still faced significant struggles. They were now seen by some as a "Genesis Lite," accused of having abandoned their progressive roots in favor of a more mainstream sound. The band's next album, *Wind & Wuthering* (1976), faced a similar critical reception—while the album was solid, it lacked the groundbreaking impact of their previous work.

Genesis' transition to stardom was not as swift or smooth as many might assume. There were internal struggles with identity, creative direction, and the balancing act of maintaining their loyal fanbase while attracting new listeners. The pressures of touring and recording were beginning to take their toll, and even as Genesis was slowly climbing toward mainstream success, the group was still finding its footing.

For Collins, however, the next few years would mark the beginning of a personal and professional transformation. As Genesis' frontman, he was growing into the charismatic and versatile performer he would later become known for. But it was clear that Genesis' future as a band would not be secure unless they could resolve their identity crisis and continue evolving as artists. Collins was ready for that challenge—and would soon be at the forefront of a new wave in Genesis' career.

In the meantime, however, the band continued to work tirelessly, refining their sound and working on their next album. It was the unrelenting drive to evolve, innovate, and push beyond their limits that would eventually transform Genesis from a progressive rock act to one of the most successful pop-rock bands of the 1980s. But the path to that success would be anything but simple.

Phil Collins' story was just beginning,

And the struggles he and Genesis faced in the years before their stardom would prove to be defining moments in the long journey ahead.

Chapter 2
THE EVOLUTION OF GENESIS – A BAND TRANSFORMED

2.1 Genesis' Breakthrough

By the mid-1970s, Genesis had firmly established itself as one of the most innovative and ambitious progressive rock bands in the world. However, despite their technical brilliance, the band was still struggling to find a mainstream audience. Their early work, which fused elements of classical music with rock, had earned them a dedicated but niche following. What Genesis needed was a breakthrough— an album that would both satisfy their progressive roots and introduce them to a broader audience.

That album came in 1973 with *Selling England by the Pound*. This album was not just another chapter in Genesis' growing catalog—it was the moment when they began to define themselves as not only a band of virtuoso musicians but as an ensemble capable of weaving intricate narratives with their music. The album's title itself was a nod to the changing social and economic landscape of England during the 1970s. Its tracks painted a vivid picture of the nation's political and cultural upheaval, juxtaposed with fantastical, often surreal imagery.

Collins' contribution to this album was nothing short of transformative. While he had already proven himself as a capable drummer, his role in Genesis was about to evolve in ways that would change the trajectory of the band's career. His drumming on *Selling England by the Pound* was both complex and nuanced, helping to elevate the album's dramatic tension. Yet it was his growing vocal ability that began to emerge as a defining characteristic of the band's sound. Songs like "Firth of Fifth" and "The Cinema Show" showcased not only his skill behind the drum kit but also his nascent talent as a vocalist, setting the stage for his eventual takeover as the band's primary frontman.

The success of *Selling England by the Pound* cemented Genesis as one of the premier progressive rock bands of the era. Its intricate compositions, poetic lyrics, and elaborate live performances captivated both critics and fans alike. The album reached No. 3 on the UK Albums Chart and was lauded for its ambitious storytelling and musical complexity. But despite its success, Genesis was still an underground band in the eyes of mainstream audiences. The band's refusal to conform to the expectations of commercial rock kept them in the margins, though they had carved out a strong niche for themselves in the progressive rock scene.

However, it was their next album, *The Lamb Lies Down on Broadway*, that would truly alter the course of Genesis' career. Released in 1974, *The Lamb* was a sprawling, two-disc concept album that told the story of a character named Rael, who embarks on a surreal journey through the underworld. The album's grandiosity and complexity pushed the boundaries of what was considered rock music at the time. Its ambitious narrative, experimental soundscapes, and fusion of diverse musical styles were a defining moment in Genesis' career.

Though the album was met with critical acclaim, *The Lamb* marked a turning point for the band. Tensions had been building within Genesis, particularly between lead singer Peter Gabriel and the other members of the band. Gabriel's increasingly theatrical approach to performance and his personal desire to explore other artistic avenues led to his departure from Genesis shortly after the album's release. This left the band in a state of flux, as they now had to figure out how to move forward without their charismatic frontman. Collins, who had always been the band's backbone with his impeccable drumming, now found himself thrust into the position of not only holding the rhythm but also filling the vocal and creative void left by Gabriel's departure.

2.2 From Progressive Rock to Pop Rock

Genesis' transition from progressive rock to a more accessible pop-rock sound is often seen as a major turning point in their career. While their early albums, such as *Nursery Cryme* and *Foxtrot*, were intricate works of art that pushed the boundaries of rock music, the mainstream success they so desperately sought eluded them. As the 1970s gave way to the 1980s, it became clear that a shift in musical direction was necessary if Genesis was going to survive and thrive in an increasingly commercial music landscape.

Collins was, by now, firmly in control of the band's direction. In the wake of Gabriel's departure, he had seamlessly taken on the role of lead vocalist, though initially with some trepidation. Collins was not interested in simply replacing Gabriel, but rather in steering the band in a direction that would both honor its past and open up new possibilities. His desire to expand the band's sound, coupled with his growing vocal confidence, led to a shift in Genesis' musical style.

The first album to reflect this new direction was *A Trick of the Tail* (1976). The album marked a departure from the extended suites and abstract storytelling of their earlier work and embraced a more concise, accessible form of songwriting. Tracks like "Dance on a Volcano" and "Los Endos" were still technically complex but had a more immediate appeal, with catchy hooks and more streamlined arrangements. Collins' vocal contributions were more prominent, and his voice—smooth yet full of emotional depth—became a central component of the band's sound.

Despite the departure from their progressive rock roots, *A Trick of the Tail* was both a critical and commercial success, reaching No. 1 on the UK Albums Chart. For the first time in their career, Genesis had produced an album that appealed to a broader audience without sacrificing the creative integrity they were known for. The success of the album proved that Collins was not only capable of filling Gabriel's shoes but was, in many ways, the key to the band's future success.

Genesis' move toward a more accessible sound continued with *Wind & Wuthering* (1976), which saw the band refine the formula established with *A Trick of the Tail*. The album featured more polished, radio-friendly tracks like "Your Own Special Way" and "Afterglow," which further solidified their transition from progressive rock to pop-rock. While the album retained much of the band's signature complexity, the emphasis was now on crafting songs that could appeal to both their loyal fanbase and a wider commercial audience.

In 1980, Genesis released *Duke*, an album that marked the culmination of their transition into pop-rock. The album's single "Turn It On Again" became one of the band's biggest hits, and its success signaled that Genesis had fully embraced a more mainstream sound. The shift was not without its detractors—many purists argued that Genesis had abandoned their progressive roots in favor of commercial success. But for Collins and the band, the decision was simple: if they wanted to reach a larger audience, they had to evolve. And evolve they did, with *Duke* propelling Genesis into the stratosphere of global pop-rock stardom.

2.3 The Impact of Collins' Leadership

By the early 1980s, Phil Collins had solidified his position as the leader of Genesis, and it was under his leadership that the band truly came into its own as a global force in pop and rock music. With his growing influence in the band, Collins helped define the sound of Genesis in the 1980s, steering the group through an era of creative and commercial success.

One of the most significant ways in which Collins shaped Genesis was through his ability to blend intricate musical arrangements with accessible pop sensibilities. His drumming, which had always been a defining element of the band's sound, remained as innovative and complex as ever, but it was now complemented by more straightforward, catchy melodies and hooks. Collins' signature sound, characterized by his crisp, distinctive drum fills and emotive vocals, became synonymous with the Genesis sound during this period.

Genesis' 1981 album, *Abacab*, was another pivotal moment in the band's evolution. The album marked a further departure from their progressive rock roots and embraced a more synthesized, electronic sound. Collins, who had begun to explore his own solo career around this time, brought his own pop-rock sensibilities to the table, influencing the album's sound. Tracks like "No Reply at All" and the title track "Abacab" showcased the band's embrace of the 1980s' burgeoning synth-pop movement, with Collins' driving rhythms and powerful vocals anchoring the songs.

Under Collins' leadership, Genesis' sound continued to evolve throughout the 1980s, culminating in the massive success of *Invisible Touch* (1986). The album's title track became one of the band's biggest hits, and its commercial success propelled Genesis into the stratosphere of mainstream pop music. "Invisible Touch" topped the charts in both the UK and the US, and its infectious melody and memorable chorus marked a new chapter in Genesis' evolution. With Collins firmly at the helm, Genesis was no longer just a progressive rock band—they had become one of the most successful and influential pop-rock acts of the decade.

Collins' leadership was not limited to his musical contributions. He was also the band's emotional anchor, managing the dynamics between the other members and maintaining a sense of unity during a time of rapid change.

His growing confidence as a frontman allowed Genesis to experiment with new sounds and explore different musical directions without losing the essence of what made them unique.

As Genesis' popularity soared, Collins' own solo career also began to take off, with hits like "In the Air Tonight" and "Against All Odds." Yet, even as he achieved success as a solo artist, Collins remained committed to Genesis, recognizing that the band's legacy was deeply intertwined with his own. His leadership helped guide Genesis through an era of immense success, and it was his vision that allowed the band to remain relevant while embracing the changing tides of the music industry.

By the end of the 1980s, Genesis had firmly cemented its place in the pantheon of rock and pop history. With Collins at the helm, they had successfully transitioned from their progressive rock roots to a more commercially viable pop-rock sound, all while maintaining the integrity and creativity that had always defined their music. The evolution of Genesis in the 1980s was not just a reflection of the changing musical landscape—it was a testament to the transformative power of Phil Collins as both a leader and an artist.

Chapter 3
SOLO AMBITIONS – A NEW PATH TO STARDOM

3.1 Taking the Leap: The First Solo Album

In the early 1980s, Phil Collins found himself at a crossroads. He had firmly established his place within Genesis, leading the band through their commercial success and embracing the role of frontman. Yet, despite the accolades and popularity, Collins felt a deep, personal desire to explore something different—a journey that would lead him to embark on his solo career.

The decision to go solo was not one that Collins took lightly. As a musician, he had always been deeply connected to the creative process, and the confines of a band dynamic were starting to feel restrictive. His growing interest in experimenting with different musical genres, his need to tell his own personal stories, and his desire to create music on his own terms led him to the realization that it was time to step out from the shadows of Genesis. Collins had the drive to carve out his own identity as an artist, separate from the legacy of the band he had helped define.

The pivotal moment came in 1981, during a period of uncertainty for Genesis. The band had been experiencing a significant shift, and their musical direction was evolving rapidly. Collins had always been the steady rhythm behind the band's sound, but with the band's success came more personal pressure and fewer opportunities to fully express himself. This was the perfect time for him to begin working on a project that would allow him to explore the deeper, more personal aspects of his artistry.

The result of this leap of faith was *Face Value*, Collins' debut solo album released in 1981. The album was both a personal catharsis and an artistic revelation. The lyrics were raw and intimate, exploring themes of love, heartbreak, and the personal turmoil that Collins was going through at the time, particularly his divorce from his first wife, Andrea. His emotions poured out in a way that was wholly new for his fans—this was not the polished, theatrical performance that characterized his work with Genesis. This was raw, unfiltered Phil Collins, speaking directly to his listeners through deeply personal music.

Musically, *Face Value* was a departure from Genesis' sound. The album embraced a more stripped-back, soulful, and at times experimental approach, blending pop, rock, and even elements of jazz and funk. The production was bold and adventurous, but it was also rooted in the intimacy of Collins' own experience. It was clear that he had stepped into a new creative territory, not bound by the constraints of band dynamics, but instead free to create whatever music spoke to him.

The album's success was undeniable. It went on to become a commercial success, reaching No. 1 on the UK Albums Chart and solidifying Collins' place as not just a drummer and band member, but a standalone artist in his own right. The critical acclaim he received for *Face Value* was a testament to his abilities as a songwriter, composer, and producer, and it marked the beginning of a new phase in his career—one where he would no longer be just the drummer from Genesis but a celebrated solo artist in his own right.

Collins' decision to go solo was a brave one, but it paid off in ways he could not have imagined. He had crossed a threshold into new creative spaces and found a voice that was his own—distinct from Genesis and yet still echoing with the musical roots he had spent years cultivating.

3.2 Defining His Sound: "In the Air Tonight"

If *Face Value* introduced Phil Collins as a solo artist, it was the single "In the Air Tonight" that solidified his place in the pop culture pantheon. The track, which remains one of Collins' most iconic songs, not only captured the essence of his new sound but also became the anthem of his personal journey.

"In the Air Tonight" was a revelation for listeners—a haunting, atmospheric piece of music that carried with it a weight of emotion, drama, and mystery. The song was eerie and sparse, with Collins' signature atmospheric drums setting the mood. The song's haunting melody, paired with the emotionally charged lyrics, struck a chord with fans on a deep level. The lyrics themselves, though somewhat cryptic, were raw and deeply emotional, hinting at personal struggles and betrayals that Collins had experienced in his personal life.

What made "In the Air Tonight" so unique, however, was its production. The song broke away from the traditional structures of pop music at the time, with Collins crafting a slow build to the explosive and unforgettable drum break that would become one of the most iconic moments in rock history. The tension created by the minimalist instrumentation and the gradual build-up in intensity was groundbreaking in pop music, and it set Collins apart from his contemporaries. The song's atmospheric, almost cinematic quality made it stand out from the radio-friendly hits of the era, and it resonated deeply with listeners who could sense the vulnerability behind Collins' performance.

There are many interpretations of the song's meaning, with some fans speculating that it's about a personal betrayal, a difficult relationship, or a moment of reckoning. Collins, however, has always kept the exact inspiration behind the song a mystery, which only added to its allure. The emotional honesty of the song, paired with its moody and experimental production, created a piece of music that transcended genre and resonated with fans in a way that few pop songs ever had.

The song was a commercial juggernaut, reaching No. 2 on the UK Singles Chart and No. 1 on the US Billboard Hot 100. "In the Air Tonight" became Collins' defining track, instantly recognizable for its haunting rhythm and emotionally charged performance. Its success helped to solidify *Face Value* as a commercial hit, and the song remains a centerpiece of Collins' career. Over the years, "In the Air Tonight" has been featured in countless films, TV shows, and advertisements, further cementing its place in popular culture.

The success of "In the Air Tonight" was more than just a hit single—it was the launchpad for Collins' career as a solo artist. The song introduced him to a whole new audience, one that recognized him as an artist capable of creating deeply emotional, genre-defying music. It showcased his versatility and ability to connect with listeners on a personal level, while also demonstrating his talent for pushing the boundaries of what pop music could be.

Through "In the Air Tonight," Collins had created a song that wasn't just a hit—it was a cultural moment, one that would remain a defining part of his legacy for years to come.

3.3 Balancing Two Worlds: Genesis and Solo Career

As Phil Collins' solo career began to soar, the challenge of balancing both his personal artistic ambitions and his commitments to Genesis became increasingly apparent. On one hand, Collins had the opportunity to explore new musical horizons with his solo work, but on the other, he was still very much a member of one of the world's most successful rock bands. Maintaining that delicate balance would prove to be both exhilarating and exhausting.

The early 1980s saw Collins juggling the demands of his solo career and Genesis, with each project demanding a significant amount of time, energy, and creative focus. After the success of *Face Value*, Collins was in high demand, both for his solo work and his role as the frontman of Genesis. He began to immerse himself in his solo music, releasing the album *Hello, I Must Be Going* in 1982, which further solidified his identity as a solo artist. Yet, despite the growing popularity of his solo music, he never fully abandoned Genesis.

In fact, Collins continued to serve as the drummer and lead vocalist of Genesis, playing an instrumental role in the band's continuing evolution. The tension between the two worlds was palpable. On one hand, Collins was trying to forge his own path as a solo artist, while on the other, he was committed to leading Genesis through the massive success of albums like *Invisible Touch* (1986) and *We Can't Dance* (1991).

The stress of maintaining both careers took its toll. As Genesis became more commercially successful in the 1980s, the band's schedules became increasingly demanding, and Collins found himself stretched thin between his solo albums, Genesis' tours, and the growing demands of his personal life. He was able to navigate these pressures for a while, but as time went on, the weight of the dual commitment began to affect his work and his personal well-being.

Despite the challenges, Collins successfully managed both careers for years, demonstrating a level of versatility and commitment to his art that was rare for artists in his position. He was a master at balancing the theatricality of Genesis with the deeply personal, introspective nature of his solo work. His ability to adapt to both worlds allowed him to thrive in both capacities, though the toll it took on him would eventually become more apparent.

In hindsight, the duality of Collins' career—being both a solo artist and a key member of Genesis—helped to solidify his place in the music world. It demonstrated that an artist could transcend the confines of a band and become a true solo icon, without losing the connection to the creative forces that made them great in the first place. However, maintaining that balance would prove to be an ongoing challenge as Collins' career continued to evolve, with both solo and Genesis demands growing ever more complex.

Chapter 4
GLOBAL STARDOM AND ARTISTIC EVOLUTION

4.1 Chart-Topping Success and Iconic Albums

By the mid-1980s, Phil Collins had already proven his exceptional abilities as a solo artist. His debut album, *Face Value*, laid the groundwork for his career, but it was his subsequent releases that truly launched him into the stratosphere of global superstardom. In 1985, he released *No Jacket Required*, an album that would become not just a commercial success but a defining moment in pop music history. The record became an international phenomenon, establishing Collins as a dominant force in the music world and showcasing his versatility as a songwriter and performer.

No Jacket Required was an album that tapped into the cultural zeitgeist of the mid-1980s. The world was emerging from the post-punk era and moving toward more accessible pop sounds, and Collins was right at the forefront of that shift. The album blended elements of pop, rock, funk, and soul, all while maintaining the distinctive melodic and lyrical sensibility that Collins had developed during his time with Genesis. Tracks like "Sussudio" and "One More Night" became instant anthems, with their infectious melodies and smooth production capturing the mood of the era. The album's sound was polished yet accessible, and its success was immediate.

Notably, *No Jacket Required* marked a departure from the introspective and moody nature of *Face Value*. While still deeply personal, the album was more upbeat, more radio-friendly, and featured more experimental production techniques. Collins had tapped into a more commercially viable pop sound, and the world was ready for it. The album went on to top the charts worldwide, hitting No. 1 on the Billboard 200 in the U.S. and the UK Albums Chart. It produced hit singles that would become iconic, including "Sussudio," "One More Night," and "Don't Lose My Number." Collins was now firmly entrenched as a global pop star, and *No Jacket Required* would go on to sell over 12 million copies worldwide.

This success was followed up in 1989 by ...*But Seriously*, an album that further solidified Collins' place as one of the biggest pop stars of the decade. The album featured a more mature sound, with deeper, more socially conscious lyrics. It was a significant departure from the more commercial pop of *No Jacket Required*, as Collins began to address personal and societal issues, including the pressures of fame, personal loss, and the struggles of relationships. The album's lead single, "Another Day in Paradise," became one of Collins' most iconic songs, with its powerful commentary on homelessness and social issues resonating deeply with listeners.

...*But Seriously* also marked a significant creative leap for Collins. The album showcased his musical diversity, incorporating everything from blues and soul to pop and rock. Tracks like "Something Happened on the Way to Heaven" and "Do You Remember?" explored the complexities of love and life, while "Another Day in Paradise" transcended the personal and spoke to global issues. The album was another commercial triumph, spending over 90 weeks on the Billboard 200 and earning multiple Grammy Awards, including Record of the Year for "Another Day in Paradise."

Both *No Jacket Required* and *...But Seriously* not only solidified Collins' place in the pantheon of pop legends but also marked a new chapter in his career. These albums demonstrated his ability to evolve artistically, to address new themes, and to connect with his audience on both an emotional and intellectual level. His success with these records gave him the freedom to experiment and grow as an artist, making him a household name and a force to be reckoned with in the music industry.

4.2 Personal Struggles and Public Triumphs

Behind the dazzling success of these albums, however, was a man grappling with the personal costs of fame. Collins' rise to superstardom came at a time when his personal life was under intense scrutiny, and the pressures of the limelight were beginning to take a toll on his well-being. His marriage to his first wife, Andrea, had begun to unravel in the late 1980s, and the public's obsession with his private life made an already difficult situation even more challenging.

In 1984, Collins and Andrea divorced, and the emotional fallout from their separation was something he poured into his music. While *No Jacket Required* had a more upbeat, commercial sound, *...But Seriously* reflected the more somber tone of his personal struggles. Songs like "Another Day in Paradise" not only dealt with global issues but also served as a metaphor for the personal turmoil Collins was experiencing at the time. The pressures of balancing his growing fame, the breakdown of his marriage, and the expectations of being a global superstar were beginning to weigh heavily on him.

Yet, despite these personal struggles, Collins continued to thrive professionally. His ability to channel his emotions into his music gave his songs a depth that resonated with fans. The public's fascination with his personal life also added a layer of intrigue to his work, making his albums feel even more intimate and personal. The dichotomy between the public perception of Collins as a superstar and the private challenges he faced made his music all the more relatable to his fans.

During this time, Collins also faced the challenges of being a public figure in an era when the media could make or break an artist. The relentless scrutiny of his every move, coupled with the constant demands of touring and recording, created a sense of isolation for Collins. Despite this, he maintained a sense of professionalism and dedication to his craft. His fans, many of whom saw him as a voice for their own struggles, continued to support him, and his popularity never wavered. The very same pressures that were weighing on him also fueled his creative fire, driving him to continue producing music that resonated on a deeply emotional level.

One of the key factors in Collins' success was his ability to evolve both personally and professionally. He was not immune to the pressures and pitfalls of fame, but he was resilient, using his struggles as material for his songs. The result was a series of albums that not only captured the spirit of the times but also reflected the complex inner life of an artist at the height of his career.

4.3 A New Era in Music and Culture

Phil Collins' success during the 1980s and early 1990s came at a time of massive cultural and musical change. The music industry was undergoing a significant transformation, with the rise of MTV, the dominance of pop stars like Michael Jackson and Madonna, and the increasing influence of electronic music. Collins, however, managed to navigate these changes while remaining true to his unique artistic vision. His music bridged genres and spoke to a wide array of listeners, from pop and rock enthusiasts to fans of soul and jazz.

Collins was also one of the first major pop stars to embrace the power of music videos, and his videos, particularly for songs like "Sussudio" and "Another Day in Paradise," became iconic in their own right. His presence on MTV helped to further establish him as a household name and expanded his fan base to a global audience. The combination of his musical talents, his charismatic performances, and his ability to connect with fans on an emotional level made Collins a pop culture icon.

Collins' influence on the music industry extended beyond his own work. He collaborated with a wide range of artists, from rock legends like Eric Clapton and Robert Plant to pop stars like Phillip Bailey and Diana Ross. His collaborations brought a new level of exposure to other musicians and helped to push the boundaries of genre. Collins was instrumental in blending elements of rock, pop, and soul, creating a sound that was distinct yet accessible to a broad audience.

As the 1990s progressed, Collins' impact on the music world was undeniable. His music continued to evolve, but the success of *No Jacket Required* and *...But Seriously* had already cemented his place as one of the defining artists of the decade. His contributions to the soundtrack of popular culture, his unique blend of personal introspection with mass appeal, and his ability to continually push the boundaries of what pop music could be made him a major influence in shaping the musical landscape.

But Collins' influence was not just confined to the music industry. His popularity helped to change the way that pop stars were perceived. He was one of the first musicians of his era to present himself as both a star and a human being, blending the larger-than-life persona of a rock icon with the vulnerability of a personal artist. This balance resonated with fans in a way that few other artists could match. Collins' music was not just for the mainstream—it was a soundtrack to the lives of everyday people, and it spoke to their experiences in a way that felt deeply personal.

In conclusion, Phil Collins' rise to global stardom and his artistic evolution in the 1980s and 1990s marked a pivotal moment in the music industry. His chart-topping success, the personal struggles he navigated, and his ability to bridge genres and cultures made him a central figure in the landscape of pop music. Collins was not just a pop star—he was an artist who understood the complexities of fame, the power of music, and the deep connection between artist and audience. His work in this period not only defined his career but also left an indelible mark on the music world for generations to come.

Chapter 5:
THE REINVENTION OF PHIL COLLINS

5.1 The Genesis Reunion and Personal Growth

By the late 1990s, Phil Collins had firmly cemented his place in the pantheon of musical icons. His commercial triumphs, particularly in the 1980s and early 1990s, had made him a household name. Yet, despite his fame and success, the years following the peak of his solo career marked a period of introspection, personal growth, and, ultimately, reinvention. The next phase of his journey would see him reconnecting with his roots—Genesis. But the reunion was not merely a nostalgia trip; it marked a more profound shift in Collins' understanding of himself, his music, and his place in the industry.

Genesis, the band that had shaped much of Collins' early career, had seen various transformations over the years. Their heyday was long behind them by the time the late 1990s rolled around. The band's sound had evolved significantly since Collins had first joined in the late 1960s, and so had the public's perception of them. The dissolution of Genesis in the early 1990s, after the band's *We Can't Dance* album, was not entirely unexpected. Members had pursued their own projects, and Collins had increasingly focused on his solo career. However, by the late 1990s, there was renewed interest in a Genesis reunion, and Collins, along with fellow members Tony Banks and Mike Rutherford, agreed to revive the band for a series of tours.

The reunion was a cathartic moment, not only for Genesis fans but for Collins as well. After years of focusing on his solo projects, his reunion with Genesis allowed him to reconnect with the roots of his musical identity. For Collins, it was an opportunity to revisit his history with the band and redefine his relationship with his music. Yet, the pressures of reconciling his solo career with the demands of the band would prove challenging. Genesis was an enormous part of his life, but the journey had been tumultuous. The reunion was both a reflection of how far the band had come and how far Collins had grown as a person.

The late 1990s marked a period of deep personal transformation for Collins. He had endured the breakdown of his first marriage, the aftermath of his own depression, and a period of intense isolation. Yet, with the Genesis reunion came a sense of renewal. Collins' personal growth was evident in the way he approached his music. He had begun to move away from the emotionally charged anthems of the past and toward a more introspective, reflective style. His reunion with Genesis was a catalyst for deeper introspection, and it influenced his subsequent work, including his solo projects. Through it all, Collins embraced his vulnerability, confronting his past in both his personal life and his music.

The success of the reunion tours proved to be both a commercial triumph and a critical affirmation of Collins' enduring relevance as a musical force. Yet, the experience also highlighted the ever-present tension between his identity as a solo artist and his role as a band member. As Collins balanced both sides of his musical career, he found himself grappling with what it meant to be a part of a collective versus an individual creative entity. This exploration of identity would become a central theme in his future work, reflecting the complexities of fame, creativity, and self-realization.

5.2 Shifting Focus: *Collateral Damage* and The Motown Influence

As Collins embraced his personal growth, his music began to evolve in ways that reflected his changing perspective on life. His 1996 album *Both Sides* marked a notable departure from the high-energy, commercial pop-rock sound that had defined much of his 1980s and early 1990s work. Instead, *Both Sides* was a deeply introspective album, marked by somber tones, complex emotions, and a more stripped-back, raw production. The album was Collins' first to feature him as the sole writer and performer of all the tracks. Gone were the days of big-band anthems and catchy pop hits; in their place was a more intimate, vulnerable side of Collins' artistry.

The title *Both Sides* itself spoke to the duality Collins was confronting in his life. On one side, he had the glitz and glamour of his career, the recognition, and the adoration of millions. On the other, he was a man facing his own emotional turmoil, trying to make sense of the complexities of his relationships, his personal challenges, and his place in the world. The album's rawness marked a sharp contrast to the polished sound of *No Jacket Required* and *...But Seriously*. The change in style mirrored the way Collins had come to terms with his personal struggles, including his divorce and his difficulties with fame.

Musically, *Both Sides* drew on a variety of influences, but perhaps most significantly, it reflected Collins' love of Motown music—a genre that had shaped his early musical sensibilities. The Motown influence can be heard in tracks like "Both Sides of the Story" and "Everyday," where the lush melodies and rhythmic sensibilities of soul and R&B provide the foundation for Collins' introspective lyrics. Motown, with its rich history of storytelling and its ability to convey complex emotions through simple, powerful melodies, offered Collins a framework through which to explore his own experiences.

The album was also significant in that it marked a shift away from the slick, synthesized production that had become synonymous with Collins' earlier work. The sound was more organic, more human, and more grounded in the soul-searching themes Collins was confronting. *Both Sides* was a cathartic expression of his own vulnerability, and it resonated with listeners who had grown to appreciate his openness and honesty. The album may not have achieved the commercial success of his previous efforts, but it was a critical success, praised for its maturity and emotional depth.

This period of introspection and artistic reinvention was a defining moment in Collins' career. *Both Sides* was not just an album but a statement—a musical manifesto of Collins' desire to return to the roots of his own musical identity, exploring deeper, more complex emotions and moving away from the formulaic pop tracks that had previously defined his sound. The exploration of Motown and soul music allowed Collins to engage with his own emotional complexities in a way that felt both personal and universal, bridging the gap between his past musical influences and his present-day struggles.

5.3 Legacy in Music: Beyond Genesis and Solo Work

As Collins continued his evolution as an artist, his legacy became more secure, not just as a pop star but as a respected and influential figure in the music world. He had helped shape the sound of the 1980s and 1990s with both Genesis and his solo career, but his influence extended far beyond those two domains. Collins' legacy lay not only in his ability to craft hit singles and albums but in his innovations in music production, his emotional depth as a songwriter, and his ability to connect with his audience on a deeply personal level.

Collins' contributions to Genesis, particularly as the band's frontman in the 1980s, were undeniable. His blend of pop sensibilities with the more progressive elements of Genesis' sound helped define the band's commercial success and expand their audience. But it was his solo work that established him as an artist in his own right. His willingness to explore complex emotions, from personal heartache to global issues, set him apart from his contemporaries and ensured his continued relevance in an ever-changing music landscape.

Perhaps one of Collins' most significant contributions to music was his approach to music production. Collins was known for his innovative use of drum machines, synthesizers, and other cutting-edge studio techniques, which helped define the sound of the 1980s. His use of the gated reverb drum sound—a technique that became one of the most iconic production features of the 1980s—was groundbreaking and set the tone for much of the pop and rock music that followed. This creative use of technology, paired with his ability to craft emotive melodies, made Collins a trailblazer in the industry.

Beyond his work with Genesis and as a solo artist, Collins' collaborations with other musicians cemented his legacy. He worked with a diverse array of artists, from Eric Clapton and Robert Plant to Celine Dion and Tina Turner. Each collaboration further demonstrated his versatility as an artist and his ability to seamlessly blend genres, from rock and pop to soul and R&B. Collins' collaborations also allowed him to influence the music of the next generation, leaving a lasting impact on the artists who came after him.

As the years passed, Collins' place in the music world became undeniable. His influence stretched beyond the confines of any one genre or era, and his ability to reinvent himself while staying true to his artistic vision ensured that his legacy would endure for decades to come. Collins' music transcended generational boundaries, and his work continued to resonate with fans old and new. Whether through his work with Genesis, his solo albums, or his collaborations with other artists, Collins had carved out a space for himself as one of the most influential figures in modern music history.

In conclusion, the reinvention of Phil Collins over the years demonstrates not only his resilience as an artist but also his commitment to personal and musical growth. From the Genesis reunion to his introspective exploration of new musical influences, Collins continually pushed the boundaries of what it meant to be an artist. His journey of transformation, while marked by personal struggles, ultimately solidified his place as one of the most influential and innovative musicians of his generation. His legacy, defined by both his chart-topping hits and his willingness to evolve, continues to shape the landscape of music today.

Chapter 6
REFLECTIONS AND THE ENDURING INFLUENCE OF PHIL COLLINS

6.1 Looking Back: The Journey to Stardom

Phil Collins' journey to superstardom is a story of resilience, evolution, and undeniable talent. From the small streets of West London, where he first picked up a pair of drumsticks, to the grand arenas of the world's biggest stages, Collins has always exemplified what it means to be an artist committed to both personal expression and universal connection. His story is a unique one—where humble beginnings collided with rare musical vision, turning him into one of the most influential and enduring figures in music history.

Collins' rise to prominence was not an accident; it was the result of years of hard work, creative ambition, and an instinctive understanding of what it took to resonate with listeners on a deep, emotional level. From his earliest days with Genesis, Collins showed an innate musicality and ability to forge connections with his audience. The British progressive rock scene of the 1970s was known for its complexity and intellectualism, but Collins' deep rhythmic sense and evolving vocals proved to be the perfect vehicle for Genesis' own musical transformation.

Genesis, a band that had originally been associated with intricate, multi-part compositions and elaborate stage shows, found a new voice with Collins at the helm. His drums were a rhythmic backbone, but it was his ability to step into the role of lead vocalist that helped the band define a new era. The success of albums like *Selling England by the Pound* and *The Lamb Lies Down on Broadway* revealed the full range of Collins' talents, from his powerful drumming to his emotive voice, which became central to Genesis' evolving identity. But it was his solo work, beginning with *Face Value* in 1981, that truly propelled him into global stardom.

Phil Collins' ability to carve out a successful solo career, even while remaining a central figure in Genesis, set him apart from his peers. His breakout single, "In the Air Tonight," became a cultural touchstone—a haunting, atmospheric track that resonated with listeners on a deep emotional level. The power of his music lay in its simplicity: stark, raw, and evocative. Collins was able to tap into universal themes of love, loss, and human vulnerability, making his music deeply relatable. By the time *No Jacket Required* and *...But Seriously* came out in the 1980s and 1990s, Collins had become an international superstar.

Despite the commercial success and accolades, Collins' career was not without its struggles. Personal challenges, including the dissolution of his marriage, his struggles with depression, and the pressures of fame, played a key role in shaping his artistic expression. But it was through these personal hardships that Collins found a new voice, one that was more introspective and reflective. The shift in his music toward more mature and vulnerable themes, particularly with *Both Sides* in the mid-1990s, marked a turning point in Collins' career, where he moved from being a pop icon to a deeply introspective artist.

His evolution over the decades demonstrates the power of reinvention. Collins proved time and again that he was willing to evolve with the times, whether by embracing new musical styles, experimenting with production techniques, or confronting personal demons. His journey from Genesis drummer to global pop sensation is the stuff of music industry legend, but it is his continued willingness to evolve and adapt that ensures his place in music history.

6.2 The Phil Collins of Today
Today, Phil Collins is a man who is both at peace with his legacy and determined to continue creating. While his

recent years have been marked by health struggles, including difficulties with his back and mobility, Collins' passion for music has not wavered. The same drive that propelled him to stardom in the 1980s and 1990s remains evident in his work today, whether through occasional live performances or studio collaborations.

While Collins is no longer the ubiquitous figure in pop culture that he once was, his impact remains felt. His music continues to resonate with new generations of listeners who were not born when he first rose to fame. Social media platforms, streaming services, and YouTube have introduced his catalog to younger audiences who may have discovered him through his iconic hits like "In the Air Tonight" or "Against All Odds." These platforms have played a crucial role in sustaining Collins' relevance, as younger audiences are exposed to his timeless music in new ways.

Collins has also continued to explore new artistic avenues, including collaborations with other musicians and participating in projects that reflect his diverse musical interests. For example, his work with *The Lion King* musical, both in the West End and on Broadway, is a testament to his ongoing influence in the world of theater and film. Collins' ability to adapt and collaborate, regardless of the medium, shows his enduring relevance as an artist. Though the days of international tours and arena shows may be behind him, his presence in the cultural zeitgeist is still significant.

In addition to his musical pursuits, Collins has also focused on his personal life, finding solace in his family and his close circle of friends. He has spoken candidly about the difficulties of living under constant public scrutiny and how he has learned to balance his personal and professional worlds. This sense of groundedness, despite his previous years of intense fame, has allowed Collins to live a more fulfilling life away from the spotlight, even as he continues to create.

While some might view Collins' recent years as a quiet period, they are instead a reflection of a man who has learned to reconcile his past with his present. In many ways, Collins is now an elder statesman of music, offering guidance and wisdom to the younger generation of artists who are influenced by his work. His role as a mentor, a collaborator, and an active participant in the music community, even in a more low-key capacity, speaks to his lasting legacy.

6.3 The Timelessness of Collins' Music

One of the most remarkable aspects of Phil Collins' career is the timelessness of his music. Though his work spans several decades, his songs continue to resonate across generations. His blend of infectious melodies, emotional depth, and lyrical honesty is as relevant today as it was when he first broke through in the early 1980s. There is something universally compelling about Collins' music, an ability to tap into the human experience in a way that transcends both genre and era.

At the heart of Collins' music is his ability to craft songs that reflect the full spectrum of human emotion. From the raw anguish of "In the Air Tonight" to the celebratory tone of "You Can't Hurry Love," Collins' catalog is marked by a remarkable emotional range. His ability to make these emotions accessible to a wide audience is perhaps his greatest strength. He never shied away from vulnerability in his music, whether in the form of his relationship struggles or his personal battles. His willingness to share these intimate aspects of his life through his art created a bond with his listeners—one based on shared experience and understanding.

Moreover, Collins' influence on the soundscape of popular music cannot be overstated. His innovative use of drum machines, synthesizers, and other technology revolutionized the pop and rock genres of the 1980s and 1990s. His use of the gated reverb drum sound, popularized on tracks like "In the Air Tonight" and "Sussudio," became iconic, setting the tone for much of the music that followed. His ability to blend progressive rock influences with pop sensibilities created a unique sound that helped define the 1980s. It was a sound that was accessible but also rich with complexity, balancing radio-friendly hooks with moments of deeper introspection.

Beyond the technical aspects of his music, Collins' songwriting remains his most enduring legacy. His songs have the rare ability to speak to listeners on a personal level. Whether tackling themes of heartbreak, self-reflection, or societal change, Collins' lyrics speak to a shared human experience. His music isn't just about entertainment—it's about creating an emotional connection with the listener, something that is at the core of why his music has endured.

Today, Collins' music is heard in multiple contexts, from movies and television to sports events and social media videos. His songs have become the backdrop to countless moments in pop culture, further cementing their timeless quality. The emotional depth and universality of his music ensure that it continues to be relevant to new audiences, no matter how much the world changes. Collins' ability to connect with listeners of all ages is a testament to the enduring power of his songwriting and performance.

As we look back on his career, it's clear that Phil Collins has left an indelible mark on the music industry. His journey from a drummer in Genesis to a global pop icon, and his ongoing relevance in today's music landscape, is a reflection of his artistry and his ability to adapt and evolve. His legacy is not defined by a single era or style but by the timeless emotional resonance of his music. Collins' ability to create songs that speak to the human condition ensures that his influence will remain for years to come, securing his place as one of the most influential and beloved musicians in history.

Conclusion:
THE ENDURING LEGACY OF A MUSICAL ICON

As we reach the end of this journey through Phil Collins' life and career, we are left with the undeniable truth that his legacy as one of the greatest musicians of all time is firmly cemented. Collins is not merely a musician; he is a cultural figure whose influence permeates both the music world and popular culture. Over the decades, he has shaped the sound of an entire era, blending genres, breaking musical boundaries, and giving voice to the deep emotions that make us human. His journey, from his early days with Genesis to his massive solo success, has been one of evolution, reinvention, and unparalleled creativity.

Phil Collins is often seen as a man of paradoxes—both the quiet, introspective artist and the global pop star who commanded arenas. His musical prowess is undeniable, yet it is his deep emotional connection to his audience that sets him apart from many of his contemporaries. His music is not just entertainment; it is a reflection of the human experience—raw, vulnerable, and deeply personal. Collins' songs transcend the fleeting nature of trends, remaining relevant to new generations of listeners who find comfort and meaning in his work.

A Musical Evolution

Collins' influence is best understood through the evolution of his sound—a journey that mirrors the changing landscape of pop and rock music. Beginning with Genesis, a band rooted in progressive rock, Collins helped usher in a new era of musical expression. His drumming became the heartbeat of the band, but it was his transition to lead vocalist that truly marked the band's transformation. Genesis' journey from complex, conceptual albums to more accessible, pop-infused rock was shaped by Collins' instincts for melody, rhythm, and songcraft. As the frontman, his voice became synonymous with the band's success, and his personal touch gave Genesis a distinct sound that would evolve and continue to shape their legacy.

When Collins embarked on his solo career, it was clear that he was not content to rest on the laurels of his band's success. His decision to step away from Genesis and establish himself as a solo artist in his own right was not merely an artistic leap—it was a reflection of his need for creative freedom. *Face Value*, his debut solo album, was a striking departure from the progressive rock world of Genesis, showcasing his ability to craft deeply personal songs that resonated on a universal level. The haunting power of "In the Air Tonight" established Collins as a solo artist with something to say—something that went beyond the confines of any particular genre.

His subsequent albums, including *No Jacket Required* and *...But Seriously,* solidified Collins' place as a global pop icon. These albums were marked by their polished production, catchy melodies, and introspective lyrics. He was able to tap into the zeitgeist of the 1980s and 1990s while still maintaining a deeply personal, vulnerable voice. Whether tackling themes of love, loss, or social issues, Collins' ability to balance universal accessibility with emotional depth helped his music stand the test of time.

Throughout his career, Collins demonstrated a remarkable capacity for reinvention. Each album was a new chapter, a fresh opportunity to explore different genres and musical landscapes. From the reflective tone of *Both Sides* to his work in musical theater with *The Lion King*, Collins consistently demonstrated his versatility and willingness to evolve as an artist. This adaptability allowed him to remain relevant in an ever-changing industry, while also pushing his own artistic boundaries.

A Voice for the Vulnerable

One of the key reasons Collins' music continues to resonate is the emotional honesty at the heart of his songwriting. Collins was never one to shy away from vulnerability—his lyrics explored the full range of human emotions, from heartache to hope, from joy to despair. Songs like "Against All Odds" and "You'll Be in My Heart" are built on themes of love, loss, and longing, and they have a way of cutting to the core of the listener's own experiences.

Collins' personal struggles—his turbulent relationships, his battles with depression, and the pressures of fame—became the fodder for much of his music. He was never afraid to expose his own pain and, in doing so, he made that pain feel universal. In a time when many musicians were focused on creating glossy, surface-level hits, Collins distinguished himself by embracing the messy, complicated nature of life. His willingness to write about his own emotional experiences created a deep connection with his fans, who saw in his songs a mirror to their own lives.

This connection to his audience is what has made his music so enduring. Collins' songs are not just about the circumstances he faced in his life—they are about the human experience itself. The themes he explored in his music—loneliness, heartbreak, love, redemption—are ones that resonate with people from all walks of life. His ability to create songs that are both intensely personal and universally relatable is one of the key reasons his music continues to be loved by generations of listeners.

The Power of Collaboration

Phil Collins' legacy is also shaped by his ability to collaborate with other artists. He was never an artist who worked in isolation, and his collaborations with other musicians helped to expand his influence. Collins' work as a producer, both for his own albums and for others, demonstrated his keen ear for sound and his ability to shape the direction of an entire project. His production on albums by artists such as Philip Bailey and Robert Plant helped to further establish him as a multifaceted musician with a deep understanding of the craft.

Moreover, Collins' collaborations with other artists, such as his work with the band Genesis and his solo endeavors, allowed him to explore different musical styles and genres. From the rhythmic complexity of *Genesis* to the smooth, soulful ballads of *No Jacket Required*, Collins was able to navigate multiple musical worlds, blending rock, pop, jazz, and R&B influences into a unique sound that was distinctly his own. His ability to move seamlessly between genres and styles has only added to his cultural relevance, allowing him to continue influencing music long after his initial rise to fame.

The Cultural Impact of Collins' Music

Phil Collins' impact extends far beyond the music industry. His work helped define the sound of an era—most notably the 1980s and 1990s—but his influence continues to be felt today. The songs that he created became anthems of the generation that grew up listening to them. Tracks like "In the Air Tonight" and "Sussudio" became inseparable from the cultural fabric of the time, soundtracking pivotal moments in movies, TV shows, and commercials. Collins' music was everywhere, and his ability to craft catchy, unforgettable tunes made him a fixture in popular culture.

Moreover, Collins' use of innovative production techniques, such as the iconic gated reverb drum sound in "In the Air

Tonight," revolutionized the sound of pop and rock music in the 1980s. His influence on both the sound of the era and the way music was produced cannot be overstated. Collins' groundbreaking work in the studio helped to create a blueprint for future musicians, influencing countless artists who followed in his footsteps.

A Legacy of Resilience

Phil Collins is also a symbol of resilience. His journey through personal and professional struggles—his divorce, health challenges, and the changing dynamics of the music industry—has been marked by perseverance and determination. He faced immense pressure from the public and the music industry, yet he continued to create, to evolve, and to inspire. Even when the music business changed in ways that made it harder for artists of his stature to maintain their relevance, Collins adapted. He was never complacent, always pushing forward, always creating.

His legacy, then, is not just one of musical achievement—it is a legacy of resilience. Collins' ability to adapt to shifting times and to continue creating music that speaks to people, despite the many obstacles he faced, is perhaps his greatest triumph. He has shown that greatness does not come from avoiding failure, but from confronting it head-on and rising above it.

The Enduring Influence of Phil Collins

In the final analysis, the music of Phil Collins is not just about the sound—it's about the emotion, the authenticity, and the timelessness of his artistry. His influence is not limited to a specific genre or era; it is woven into the very fabric of modern music. From his groundbreaking work with Genesis to his iconic solo hits, Collins' music continues to inspire, to comfort, and to move audiences around the world.

Phil Collins is more than a musician—he is an icon whose contributions to music will be felt for generations to come. His legacy is not defined by a single song, album, or moment in time, but by the lasting emotional connection he forged with his listeners. It is in the universal themes of his music, the emotional depth of his lyrics, and the timeless nature of his sound that Collins' true legacy lies. His place in the pantheon of musical greats is secure, and his influence on both the past and future of music remains immeasurable.

Phil Collins' music will always be there, playing in the background of our lives, serving as the soundtrack to our own journeys, and reminding us that through every high, every low, and every twist in the road, the music remains.

Printed in Dunstable, United Kingdom